BUILDING THE CHATEAU MONTEBELLO

Aerial view of the Chateau Montebello complex — the six-winged Log Chateau, the complex horseshoe-and-bar garage, the curved Cedar Hall staff quarters. The small bay at the right is the marina with its log boathouse next to the enclosed swimming pool with enormous skylights.

BUILDING
THE CHATEAU MONTEBELLO

Allan and Doris Muir
in collaboration with Victor Nymark

Muir Publishing Company Ltd
Gardenvale, Que., Canada HX9 1B0

1st printing, July 1980
Printed and bound in Canada by Apex Press Limited

2nd printing, April 1985
Printed and bound in Canada by Harpell's Press Cooperative

ISBN 0-919231-00-4 pbk
ISBN 0-919231-01-2

Contents

PART ONE
Papineau in Montebello   9

PART TWO
Building the Chateau Montebello   15

PART THREE
Life at the Seigniory Club   79

Epilogue   140

Bibliography   142

Recommended Books on Log Building   143

Moonlight on Lake Papineau, Lucerne-in-Quebec

In the beginning was the land . . .

And it was called La Seigniory de La Petite Nation. The Algonquin Indians lived there. They took care of the land. It was a gift to them from the Great Spirit. They respected the gift.

And then the white man came and the land was finally ceded to the Papineau family — a name famed in Canadian history. The Papineaus also respected the land and took steps to settle it. They adopted the French 'Seigneurial' system, which was primarily based on family and agricultural development.

The most famous Papineau, Louis-Joseph, who led the 1837 Rebellion against British rule, was finally pardoned in 1845 and returned to his Seigniory de La Petite Nation where, apart from a brief and unhappy return to politics for two years, he spent the rest of his life at his beloved Seigniory, happy amidst his books and famous visitors.

In 1929, members of the Lucerne-in-Quebec Community Association bought most of the Seigniory de La Petite Nation from descendants of the Papineau family and the Seigniory Club was born. The new Seigniory Club accepted an idea, a vision of what the land could be.

Respect for the land and the proper use of its natural resources has led to one of the world's great masterpieces of total recreational management with the least possible damage to the environment. Everything at the Chateau Montebello looks as if it belongs there. Everything harmonizes. Nothing offends. The result is peace. It is a lovely refreshing place to visit. It is a joy to see so much used so wisely and so well. The land is used, but not abused. We are glad today for the men who had the vision.

Praised be the Great Spirit!

Lucerne-in-Quebec Community Association Limited
Montebello, Que.
Photograph No......3
Date Taken......Feb.26th 1930
Title......Chateau.

*The illustrious Papineau Manor, Headquarters of
the Seigniory Club.*

PART ONE

Papineau in Montebello

Louis-Joseph Papineau

The Log Chateau at Montebello, Quebec, Canada, is the largest log structure in the world. However, its fame is not only because of its size or the oddity of its construction. Other reasons are the gentle charm about the place, the homespun type of furnishings, the trees that group close about its wings, the fun of summer and winter sports and the beauty of the surrounding forests.

And not the least of these is the charming Manor House, set high on a wooded promontory east of the Log Chateau, around which centered the old Seigniory de la Petite Nation (named after the Little Nation Indians of the Algonquin Tribe) who roamed in the vicinity. The Manor House and the Log Chateau, and many other log buildings, now constitute what is known as the Seigniory Club, a unique organization which occupies about 104 square miles of territory which once formed part of the famous old Seigniory. The Seigniory Club is dedicated to preserving the forested property in its natural habitat and the only buildings allowed on the property must blend in with the forest and lakes and streams. A fuller description of the Seigniory Club and its aims appears later in this book.

The first owner of the Seigniory de La Petite Nation was Monseigneur de Montmorency-Laval, Bishop of Laval, a prelate who owned two other seigniories. (Coincidentally enough, at the present time of writing, Bishop Laval has just been beatified by Pope John Paul II — the first step towards canonization as a saint). Bishop Laval was ceded the Seigniory de La Petite Nation by the Company of One Hundred Associates in 1674. Its most famous seigneur was Louis-Joseph Papineau, a name greatly

honored in the province of Quebec. These two names alone invoke a moving picture of past times, beginning with the austere prelate who exercised temporal as well as spiritual control over the infant colony, and closing with the great reformer, who was called a rebel in his day and a patriot in ours.

What a pageant of history could illuminate the development of the colony from start to finish. First came the missionaries, for they preceded the explorers in many cases and often died martyrs' deaths, then the adventurous travellers themselves, the fur traders and coureurs de bois, and always, the Indians. Up and down the Ottawa River, an artery giving access to the interior of Canada, the Indians of the Little Nation of the Algonquin Tribe, saw the passing canoes of paleface and redskins.

Since Bishop Laval was busy with his ecclesiastical duties and the development of his two other seigniories, La Petite Nation did not see any attempt at colonization or development for another century or more. Finally, the Bishop gave the land to the great Seminary of Quebec, which he had founded. In 1801 it was acquired by the Papineau family in return for notarial services rendered to the Seminary. That year two-fifths and three years later three-fifths, were ceded to Joseph Papineau, a member of the Legislative Assembly of Lower Canada. It was then that the active history of the Seigniory de La Petite Nation began.

The seigneurial system was similar in a sense to the feudal system, that structure of mutual loyalties and responsibilities on whose pyramid the power of France was built. In crossing the Atlantic it suffered a sea change and developed a French Canadian counterpart or system 'Seigneurial'. To some individual

Reception Hall, Seigniory Club, Papineau Manor.

above the average in blood and intelligence, the King of France would grant a tract of wilderness, often huge, and to him issued patents of nobility if he was not already so distinguished. In return, the Seigneur was pledged to clear his land and pay fidelty and homage to his sovereign.

The Seigneur, land poor and sometimes proud, now gathered to his estate the less fortunate who had neither land nor pride and parcelled it out among them. What he was to his sovereign, his tenants (called censitaires) were to him. His duty was to protect and counsel, captain the fort against the Indians, and build a mill for grain. Theirs was to clear the land, defend the fort and multiply. (This information about the Seigneurial system is explained more fully in the book "Quebec, Montreal & Ottawa" by T. M. Longstreth.)

Upon acquiring the Seigniory de La Petite Nation, Joseph Papineau deserted the comfort and gaiety of the city for a region cut off from the world and roamed over by Indians who were often quite bothersome. A nucleus of settlement gathered round the first Manor House built in 1805 at Arosen Island in the Ottawa River opposite the present prosperous village of Papineauville. This was occupied by the family until destroyed by fire some thirty years later. This first manor house was built of log construction. The years that followed saw the influx of more settlers and the establishment of many little communities still there today. Over the years the Seigniory de La Petite Nation dwindled in size from its previous boundaries which included the present villages of Papineauville, Montebello, Fassett, Plaisance, St. Andre Avelin, and Notre Dame de la Paix. The heart of it remains, however, now embraced by the boundaries of Le Chateau Montebello, over a hundred square miles in area, extending inland from the village of Montebello.

It was one of Joseph Papineau's sons, the famous Louis-Joseph (to whom he afterwards transferred ownership of the property) whose political career in the first quarter of the nineteenth century shook the structure of Canada almost to its foundations. The Rebellions in Upper and Lower Canada of 1837-38 are of little importance in the general scheme of world history and it is not our intention to dwell on them here. Louis-Joseph Papineau feared the merchants and fur traders. He longed to restore the old agricultural, seigniory system upon which the power of France had been built and which seemed to him to contain the really worthwhile values in life. But the merchants were too powerful and Papineau's own indecisive character, more suited to study and philosophy, led to his downfall.

The story of the Rebellion of 1837 is well-known to Canadians. Papineau always declared that he was no more responsible for the armed uprising than others of his colleagues. After a skirmish with government troops at St. Denis, where several lives were lost, including that of his closest friend, Papineau fled to the United States, later going to Paris where he remained until 1845. An amnesty was then declared and he returned to Canada and the Seigniory of Montebello, where he settled down to the life of a country gentleman.

Within a year or two, Papineau was returned to the Canadian Parliament, remaining a member until 1854. But he was no longer in the forefront with reforms, for these had been accomplished and responsible Government was in force. He abandoned politics in 1854 and retired to the Seigniory de La Petite Nation. The Seigniory then began to flourish.

The Manor House was built in 1850 when Papineau was sixty-four. It is large and square and three storeys in height with dormer windows in the third. Its squareness is masked by turrets, chateau style, on the corners facing the Ottawa River. A stone tower, which Papineau built for the safety of the library, is to the right of the main entrance. A large central hall without a staircase divides the house in two, French doors opening at each end. In the turrets, quaint, circular staircases lead to the upper floors. The Manor is beautifully decorated and furnished in Empire style, restored as nearly as possible to what it was in Papineau's lifetime.

And here, until his death in 1871, Louis-Joseph Papineau spent the happiest years of his life. After Papineau's death the Seigniory was divided between his children and the chateau, together with the domain which extended some distance from chemin Azelie, past Saint Hyacinthe Road, was acquired from the direct representatives of one of the branches. From it has sprung this ideal vacation land with its roads and golf course carved from the solid rock and primeval forest and its buildings of unique design and architecture that formed the Lucerne-in-Quebec Community Association Limited, sponsored by the Canadian Pacific Railway Company, and later to be known as the Seigniory Club.

The famous spiral staircase, Seigniory Club, Papineau Manor.

Papineau in Montebello

A Chronological Summary

1674   The Seigniory de La Petite Nation is ceded by the Company of One Hundred Associates to Bishop Laval.

1690   Bishop Laval cedes all his holdings, including the Seigniory de La Petite Nation, to the Seminary of Quebec.

1775-76 Joseph Papineau, during the American invasion, carried despatches concealed in a walking stick for the British forces from Montreal to Quebec.

1802   Notary Joseph Papineau receives as payment of monies due him by the Seminary of Quebec, 2/5ths of La Petite Nation.

1804   Joseph Papineau acquires the remaining 3/5ths of the Seigniory.

1805   Joseph Papineau built a manor house of logs at Arosen Island opposite Papineauville about four miles from Montebello.

1810   Joseph Papineau took up residence at the Seigniory and brought in the first nineteen settlers. Papineau built a mill and proceeded with other work of settlement.

1817   Joseph Papineau cedes to his son, Louis-Joseph, the Petite Nation Seigniory, while reserving for another of his sons, Denis-Benjamin, the back territory of Plaisance.

1819   First manor house burned down and Papineau family moved to a house which stood two or three miles below present village of Fassett.

1820-21 Beginnings of colonization. Construction of some 20 houses.

1821   Blessing of a chapel.

1826   Construction of a saw mill. A crude mill had been in existence for two years already. Most of this work was done by Joseph Papineau and his son Denis-Benjamin, while Louis-Joseph Papineau, in Quebec and Montreal, was busy fighting a proposed Union Bill which would unite Upper and Lower Canada and abolish the French language.

1831   Canonical erection of the parish of Notre Dame de Bonsecours de La Petite Nation. The same year rebellion broke out in Montreal with Louis-Joseph Papineau considered its nominal leader. Asiatic Cholera also afflicted the Colony, the incidence of which was blamed by Louis-Joseph Papineau on the subservience of the Quebec government to Montreal merchants who opposed quarantine. Louis-Joseph Papineau's fight was really to restore the old agricultural, seigniory system against the interests of the traders and merchants.

1837   Open rebellion in the two Canadas. Leaders were William Lyon Mackenzie (grandfather of Mackenzie King) and Louis-Joseph Papineau. Warrants issued for arrest of Papineau. With a number of friends he left for the United States where he found considerable sympathy for his cause. Papineau stayed in Saratoga, N.Y., for some time. Then he went into exile in Paris where he was active in literary and political circles. In 1845 Papineau was granted amnesty and returned to Montreal. Papineau was now anti-British, against the monarchy and suspicious of cooperation with the British. He never regained power in politics but concentrated on his family and the Seigniory de La Petite Nation.

A Seigniory Club drawing room, Papineau Manor.

The famous Library Tower, Papineau Manor. Here, Papineau kept his six thousand volumes.

1846	Louis-Joseph settled on La Petite Nation in the house of the blacksmith Fortin. From there, he led the clearing of the mount where he wished to build the Manor House. The digging of the cellars was begun about this time. He brought in more settlers, saw to the building of roads, and generously helped churches and schools.
1850	Although he returned to politics his heart was in the Seigniory and he built the Manor House, modelled on the plans of the ancient Chateau DeBlois in France. He directed the building operations himself and it took three or four years to build. The old square tower which resembled a fort was never used as such, but as the storehouse for his famous library, connected to the main house by a corridor. The little red brick building of Gothic design standing near what is now the main gate (but in the old days was a rear entrance leading to the Manor House), was built as a granary for the seed harvested on the estate.
1851	The Papineaus took possession of their Manor House though it was not quite completed.
1851-59	Exquisite furnishing acquired during this period.
1853	Main body of Manor House completed. The name of Monte-Bello is chosen.
1855	The blessing of the funeral chapel. Concession of land to 400 settlers. In the next four years, 300 more will come and settle on the Seigniory. Papineau traces the streets of the village and some new country lanes.
1871	Louis-Joseph Papineau died at age of 85 and was buried in the crypt with other members of the family. *(Credit for much of the above data is due to Roger Le Moine, of the University of Ottawa, and to the records of the Seigniory Club, Montebello.)*

Lucerne-in-Quebec Community Assoc.Ltd
Montebello, Que.
Photograph. No..73
Date Ta¨.... July 2ⁿᵈ./30
Title..Log Lodge General View from
Riverfront

The total perimeter of the Log Chateau is 2000 feet.
The length of each bedroom wing is 161 feet.

PART TWO

Building the Chateau Montebello

The creation of the Chateau Montebello in 1930 was tremendous news fifty years ago. The romance and history of its site, its huge area, its facilities for every known summer and winter sports, the unique log buildings, miles of roads, water supply and other amenities of modern life in a wilderness setting, made it almost a seventh wonder of the world — certainly of the Canadian world. Canadians woke up to the fact that the largest resort in the North American continent was planned for the North Shore of the Ottawa River and the forest area behind Montebello. They were further startled when they were told the building was to take place at a scale and speed that challenged credulity.

"The publicity given this undertaking naturally attracted crowds," wrote Harold Lawson, the Montreal architect who designed the immense project, "especially on weekends. From Montreal, Ottawa and other places visitors came by train and car over dusty roads to examine the interesting construction and to marvel at the rapid progress of the work. A perusal of the newspaper files of that period reveals an abundance of adjectives and superlatives that would do credit to a circus announcement. The buildings' construction — the whole performance, if you will — contained from beginning to end all the drama and interest of a three-ring circus."

The three buildings that really caught the public's imagination were the huge Log Chateau, the immense garage, and Cedar Hall, a residence building for the staff. They were all to be built of logs, a tremendous novelty in itself, but their enormous size really boggled the mind. On top of all that, they were being built at one time with a miraculous speed never before, it is believed, achieved in building construction.

As the buildings neared completion the excitement intensified until the grand opening of the Log Chateau on July 1st, 1930. The impossible had been accomplished. Three huge buildings embodying a new technique (then new to this country) and containing altogether 4,000,000 cubic feet, had been constructed within a period of four months. "Let me repeat," wrote Architect Lawson, with justifiable pride, *only four months!"*

How was it done? Such a project in a sparsely populated area obviously required preliminary preparations not needed in a city. Before any construction could begin, a spur line from the Canadian Pacific Railway Company had to be built to the site and a temporary construction village erected.

The spur line, 3,700 feet long, was a prime necessity, for in those days roads of the North Shore of the Ottawa River were totally unfit for heavy traffic and almost all building materials had to come by rail. During the course of construction vast quantities of materials rolled in according to pre-arranged schedules until 1,200 cars had been unloaded.

Fifteen temporary buildings were built to serve as adjuncts for construction purposes. There was a commissary and bunk houses. The commissary provided the workmen with three meals a day until at the height of construction over 3,500 men had to be fed. Sleeping arrangements at the site included the bunk houses, 14 Colonist cars, a sleeping camp at Montebello and another at Fassett. After the opening of the Log Chateau on July 1st, 1930, all these temporary buildings within the grounds disappeared almost overnight.

Truly, the tiny village of Montebello in Quebec was one of the few bright spots in the bleak employment picture of 1930.

The Chateau Montebello, built as a private members club, was the dream of H. M. Saddlemire, a Swiss-American who had already built a similar, though smaller, club in Maine called Lucerne-in-Maine. The Quebec project was called Lucerne-in-Quebec and the club's name was the Lucerne-in-Quebec Community Association Limited. More details will be given about the club's membership, activities, dues and sponsorship later in this book. It is enough to say here that it was a millionnaire's dream and only a millionnaire could have afforded such an ostentatious project during the depression years.

The laborers — many local residents, still more from depressed areas across Canada, and many from European countries — worked a 10-hour day. As the deadline approached two 12-hour shifts were implemented. Many of the workmen continued to work at the Chateau after it was completed because there was much more to be done, including building the club member's homes, and some of the original workmen are still employed by the Chateau today. Any kind of money in those days was more than welcome and it is said that plumber's apprentices were paid 20 cents an hour, as were ordinary, laborers while others were paid up to 55 cents an hour for the highest salary — first class carpenters. But in those days two pounds of beef cost only 25 cents and butter was 15 cents a pound, so the men were able to get by quite nicely.

The Master Log Builder of the Chateau Montebello was Victor Nymark who came by his job in a truly enterprising way. Victor Nymark is probably the world's greatest log builder. He supervised the log construction of the Chateau Montebello, Alpine Inn, Nymark Lodge, St. Francis of the Birds church, and innumerable private log residences. He arrived in Canada from Finland in 1924 with $25 in his pocket, couldn't speak English or French, but landed a job his very first day in the country.

"I was walking down Dorchester Boulevard in Montreal," he recalls, "and I saw a man cutting down a beautiful tree. I thought to myself there must be some reason for doing that — maybe some building here. So I went in the gate and started talking to him the best I could and I got to understand that the buildings there had to be torn down to make bigger buildings. So I asked him who was the owner and I went to see him. I got the job to start to take windows and doors out. By the end of the week I was hiring Canadians to work on the job."

It sounds easy, but Nymark was already a master log builder when he left Finland. He completed his first log building in Finland in 1917. He was only 16 years old. He studied hard and became a master builder in Finland. "In Finland you have to know not only log building but just everything in construction." When he came over to Canada in 1924 he had his papers translated into English so that when he showed them he could get a job.

A shrewd man, Nymark realized when the Great Depression hit that the only people who could afford his skills were millionaires. So he started promoting that idea. "I thought to myself they have to be millionaires or I don't spend my time." He built only for the owners of huge corporations like the Montreal Star, The St. Lawrence Sugar Refinery, rich stockbrokers, and so on. One day he read in the newspaper that the Canadian Pacific Railway Company was going to build a big log project in Montebello, based on an idea from an enterprising American, so he went to see these people. "They didn't know where to turn to for a master log builder," says Nymark, "so I got the job."

(*Editor's note*: The full story of Victor Nymark's association with the Chateau Montebello is contained in our publication, *The Log Home Guide for Builders & Buyers, 1978*).

Nymark had about 800 log builders working under him — mostly men from Europe who were accustomed to building with Scandinavian techniques. What is seldom mentioned in stories about the Chateau Montebello is that these men worked with axes and scribers: there were no chainsaws available in those days!

"I went there to Montebello in about the middle of March," says Nymark. "There was just a big swamp. You were jumping from one stump to another. We started in the middle of March and we had the Chateau open for the first of July. And all that work was hand work. My log builders got paid 50 cents an hour."

Like any other building, the Log Chateau has a high stone and concrete basement. Above this basement all resemblance to usual construction ceases, for the upper stories of the six wings and rotunda of the Log Chateau have log walls. The large horseshoe shaped garage with its center court and jutting wings, except for one portion, is a one-storey log structure. Cedar Hall, the staff residence, is a two storey log building. All have roofs covered with hand-split western red cedar shakes.

Excavation for the Log Chateau began on March 15th, 1930. Skeleton drawings only were available and instead of starting at the center and working outward, Harold Lawson pointed out, "which would have been easier, the work was begun at the southwest wing, where all the kitchen equipment was installed, other sections following in rapid order as the working crews increased in number." Log work started immediately as soon as the basement of each wing was completed.

The first log on the garage was set on April 7th, 1930, and all log work throughout the project was completed by June 7th. The progress photographs shown in this book give an excellent indication of the appearance of the Log Chateau with logs in place and the roofs in various stages of completion.

The plans for the various buildings were rushed to completion as the various buildings went up. In fact, in some cases, the log builders didn't receive any plans until after they had erected the logs. Everything was being done in a mad dash and, surprisingly, everything turned out well. There were no serious accidents despite the weight and length of some of the huge logs.

Nymark recalls that "during the first month of construction four carloads of logs were received daily plus all other construction materials."

All logs (of western red cedar) were first placed on rows of skids to keep them clean and for orderly assembly-line cutting, grooving and scribing. This skilled work was done mostly by the European log builders who had learned their trade in the Scandinavian countries and Russia. They were really skilled in the technique used in these buildings, so different from the crude methods used in most pioneer cabins. This technique was similar to that which had been used in Russia and Scandinavian countries for hundreds of years and proven solid and sound, wind and weather tight, and with excellent insulating qualities against heat or cold.

Ten thousand western red cedars were used on the first three buildings which, if placed end to end, would stretch for a distance of forty miles. Taking into consideration the vast number of logs used, and as each required considerable hand labor of a precise nature, and needed moving at least half a dozen times before incorporation in the building, it is remarkable that so much work could have been done in so short a time. In the log work, as in every other trade, in spite of the need for speed, highest standards were rigidly enforced from beginning to end.

The work of preparing the site must have been a miserable experience for those involved. Trees had to be cut away and excess snow cleared to make an early start in the spring and also to lay out the lines of the foundations. On February 26, 1930, a steam shovel was used to dig the foundation of the garage. The site was a quagmire and much water had to be drained away. By March 17 the foundation walls of the garage were partially completed and bolts were sticking up from the concrete walls to receive the logs. On March 17, also, the site of Cedar Hall, the staff residence, was cleared of trees and excess snow.

On April 3, the Log Chateau and basements were well advanced with stone arches to form part of the diningroom. The log work was about to begin. On this date also the garage foundation was completed. In the pictures of all this work can be seen the old-fashioned steel-wheeled carts and horses and wagons. Form work for Cedar Hall was well underway. The site was like a swamp with water being pumped away furiously. Boardwalks were needed everywhere.

April 3 was also the magical date when the first load of logs came in by railcar. The logs were unloaded onto log runways for sorting, cutting and scribing. The elevated runways kept the logs clean and easier to work at.

In the early spring when the snow was melting it was hardly possible to walk in from the main highway to the various sites. Many carloads of cement and rubble stone, and seemingly endless truck loads (and wagon loads driven by local farmers) of gravel from local pits, had to be brought in to form the foundations and make a road bed where trucks would not stick and workmen wouldn't sink up to their waists in the slushy terrain. At the same time, in a remarkably orderly timetable, logs, lumber and other structural materials from far and near arrived by way of the spur line.

On April 10, a beautiful sunny day, logs began to be stacked in earnest alongside the various foundations and the first day of log construction on the Log Chateau began. The tempo of the log work increased greatly within a few days with the arrival of more men and a shift to round-the-clock operation. Simultaneously, on April 15, the floor system of Cedar Hall was well under way with floor joists and the subflooring being laid. On this day also the log work on the garage was up to the eaves in most parts and ready for the roof structure.

On May 1, twenty days after construction began, one wing of the lodge was nearly completed. "The log alignment was perfect," says Nymark. Picture no. 31 shows the beautiful work performed. The entrance in the log wing is made prominent by the big posts, braces and rafters, all from round logs. Note the spline on the side of the window on the top floor. The spline fits into the groove in the end of the logs and allows for shrinkage and settling. The window frame is nailed on to the spline to hold it in place and still allow for shrinkage of the logs.

On May 1 (picture no. 33), the log joists for the diningroom balcony protruded over the stone foundation wall. A log builder armed only with an axe and scribers carved out that job. On the same day, the log work was almost completed at Cedar Hall and the rafters were being installed. The way the incredibly diversified work proceeded simultaneously at the different sites was little short of miraculous. For on this same day also, the stone foundation on Wing "C" was completed and the log work started.

"The 800 men under my direction," says Nymark, "had to unload the cars and bring them all to the buildings. We had it arranged that the work never stopped. We worked 24 hours straight. When one man stopped working another man started. We worked all round, wherever we could place men. The whole place went up evenly.

"I always put one new man with one older one. As we got going more, I took more men and continued to do this. I divided them into groups of 50 men with one man in charge of each group. You had to make sure they knew what they were doing. I was working long hours myself. Once you have all those men you have to think what you need ahead of time for tomorrow because you have limited time and you can not be held up by anything. Plan everything in advance so you know what you need for the next weekend. That was the major thing I had to do."

The rotunda in the Log Chateau is a marvellously complex piece of work. The six wings extend from a center core. The center core is the site of the amazing six-sided fireplace. On May 1 the massive forms had been completed and workmen were ready to pour concrete. Steel rods reinforce the concrete beams and floor. While the concrete floor was still soft wood and firring strips were set into the soft concrete and then the oak floor was laid.

The interior of this central core — a hexagonal lounge — is monumental in scale and of most interesting character. The focal point, from which the entire scheme radiates, is a colossal, hexa-

gonal chimney. There is a deep stone fireplace upon each of the six faces. These fireplaces are raised two steps above the lounge level and are crowned with a running bracketted cornice. The fire-dogs, grates and gates are of wrought iron, and the entire fireplace to the top of the mantleshelf is of cut stone. Above, running clear up to the main cut stone cornice which supports the ends of the main roof truss, the walls of the hexagonal mass are of random rubble of varied texture and color. In each of these is a flat niche crowned by a pointed Gothic arch and from the centre of each niche is suspended from a wrought iron bracket of pleasing design, a large and well designed wrought iron lantern.

The ceiling of the lounge has been made of open-rafter construction and galleries run completely around at the second and third storey level. With ample daylight, wonderfully comfortable furnishings and plently of supplementary lighting fixtures, the lounge has proved to be one of the most popular rooms of its type on the continent.

When we asked Victor Nymark about the difficulties encountered in constructing the open-rafter ceiling in the lounge area, he answered with his customary shy and modest attitude, "Oh, it wasn't so bad. Those logs were almost whole trees but they weren't all that heavy. Three fellows could hold them in place. If I remember correctly they are a bit over 60 feet in length. We had a little crane that went around lifting up the logs for the men. After that, the men had to take it by hand. We prett y much lifted them by hand once we got them on to the scaffold."

Meanwhile, outside, men were swarming over the huge spider's web structure of logs like ants on an anthill. The ends of the logs were cut to different lengths and painted to give a rustic appearance. At night, hundreds of lights made a fairy wonderland with what appeared to be little gnomes roaming over it with logs on their shoulders. In spite of much of the misery due to the cold weather, the mud and snow, men who worked on the various buildings still remember the experience as one of the most fascinating of their lives.

The foundation of the boiler room wing was now in place and the logs were going up fast. The crane used to lift the lounge rafters — the only crane used in the entire construction, in fact — was used to lift building materials and logs on the various buildings, such as the boiler room. The whole complex of Log Chateau, garage, and Cedar Hall and other buildings were all heated by steam from the boilers installed in the basement of this wing. A driveway is located at the base of this wing granting access to the main entrance. A movie theatre is located on the second floor of the boiler wing with an entrance from the balcony in the lobby.

On all wings of the Log Chateau there are lumber rafters with log ends for effect. Originally all of the logs were doweled but to speed up the work spikes dipped in oil were used. The spikes were countersunk to avoid hang-up.

One of the big problems was that the town of Montebello did not have a complete sewer system at the time and could not handle the Log Chateau. A separate sewer line and tile bed had to be laid.

To reinforce long walls vertical posts were erected on both sides of the log walls and held together with bolts placed in oblong holes to allow for shrinkage. Picture no. 56 shows two posts on each side with the bolt in between so that the horizontal logs can go down as shrinkage takes place. One thing missing in this picture is a steel plate or large washer under the head of the bolt to make it easier to come down with shrinkage.

By May 22, the scaffolding was almost ready to be taken away and finishing touches undertaken. Building materials were being cleared away. The main job remaining to be done was to put up the 500,000 cedar shakes.

By June 2, very little construction work remained to be done except on the diningroom wing and the center part of the lodge.

Nymark said the most difficult part of the whole project was the roof structure of the rotunda, not just the log rafters but the beam trusses above the chimney across the whole roof area. The rafter logs tie in at the upper ends to other logs circling the chimney. None of the logs rested against the chimney. The chimney, by the way, is sixty-six feet high!

June 23 was the date when clearing up the site was begun. Nothing that could be used was wasted. Large logs and log ends were used to build the gate house. There were so many men there was always some project to do and lots of left-over materials with which to do it. This left only one week before the grand opening on July 1 and landscaping, painting, mud and dirt removal, dismantling the temporary bunkhouses and tents, etc., meant no let-up on the round-the-clock pace which had been maintained from the beginning. There were many "comedies of errors" in those last seven days and we feel it would be interesting to recite some of them as remembered by H. L. Furst, the late, but extremely popular, secretary of the Seigniory Club. Mr. Hurst's account will also open our eyes to other facets of the ambitious project.

"Just prior to the opening," Mr. Furst wrote in an article in "Le Seigneur", "there was confusion and there was mud everywhere; furniture, china and cutlery were being delivered at the back entrance as the first guests came in the main door; a troupe of entertainers engaged for the cabinet acts for the opening dance walked the plank over a sea of mud to the "D" wing entrance. The Log Chateau, its foundations and its immediate surroundings were in a sense synthetic and grew like some strange culture overnight in a welter of clay where it seemed impossible for anything to take shape."

In that first day of July, 1930, wrote Mr. Furst, people came to see and admire. If that same group were to assemble today what a metamorphosis would be seen in matters great and small! There are changes material and immaterial; maturity has given place to rawness; a past of a genial human sort has come where before there was only a shapeless and almost fantastic future.

After the Club property was purchased in the autumn of 1929 there followed the broad outline of membership plans, the scheme of arrangement for the various services, etc. Then construction work started and was finished in a speed which is considered to be a first in terms of architectural records. The Log Chateau, Manor House renovations, Garage, Cedar Hall, Tennis Courts and a temporary 9-hole golf course (in the vicinity of the Horse Show Grounds) as well as some of the roads in the Community were completed and the Club was formally opened on July 1, 1930. At that time the 18 holes of the main golf course had been cleared and graded and only a temporary water system was serving the Log Chateau.

The balance of the building and other services were, according to the program, to be completed by the following year. Much of the work was carried on during the fall and winter of 1930 and 1931: by the end of 1931, the Entrance Gate, Swimming Pool, Boathouse, Sports Club House, dredging of the boat basin, the riprapping of the shore line of the Ottawa River, main golf course, balance of community roads, road to Lake Commandant, Fish Hatchery and the water system, serving both the Club and the village of Montebello, were completed. Artificial ice for the curling rink was not originally contemplated but later this was added, with two sheets completed by the end of 1931. Due to subsequent interest in curling, two extra sheets were added in 1938.

"During the planning period," wrote Mr. Furst, "careful study was given to the hundreds of details involved in the development. It was quite a problem, for instance, to decide where the road to Lake Commandant was to be located. At that time a very poor gravel parish road ran from Montebello northward seven miles to the location of the present Entrance Cabin to the forest and beyond that point the country was completely bush land. If it was chosen to extend this road, a route had to be found to the lake. The alternate road considered was by way of the village of Fassett and then to cut north following the Salmon River to Pine Cottage and then to the Lake. However, the point that weighed heavily in deciding the final location was the fact that a spring, tested for a year, to form the water supply for the fish hatchery, was found to be satisfactory and the hatchery location was fixed on the present road.

"Another important decision in connection with the planning was whether to make the Log Chateau's main fireplace a large affair with six openings or put in six separate fireplaces, as was done, the former idea proving impracticable from many points of view.

"Also, when the Log Chateau was originally designed, no third floor rooms had been intended and actually they were only added while the building was under construction. This proved an important addition as the Club could not have operated satisfactorily from a financial point of view without the additional space."

In 1930, when the Seigniory Club took over the 104 square mile property, it had an encumbrance of about 30,000 cords of wood to be cut and taken off by the previous owners. To haul this wood out they had built a railway that ran deep into the territory and constituted a fire hazard. After about eight years this cutting operation was completed and the railway dismantled, providing the club management with a better chance to improve the territory and restore it to its original beauty.

1931 saw trees planted in open areas throughout the territory and in areas adjacent to the old railway line. This was done not only for embellishment but to increase the value of the estate, to slow up the runoff so as to get a steadier flow of water in the streams. The provision of this better forest cover gradually lowered the water temperatures in streams and created a better habitat for game fish.

QUANTITIES OF MATERIALS USED IN BUILDING THE CHATEAU MONTEBELLO

The quantities of materials incorporated in these structures stagger the imagination. Seventeen carloads, or a total of 500,000 hand split cedar shakes were used on the roofs, this being the largest order ever shipped across the continent for a single job.

There were altogether 53 miles of plumbing and heating pipes, 843 fixtures and 700 Radiators. Concurrently with other mechanical trades or as soon as there was space, 7,600 sprinkler heads were carefully installed in prearranged patterns to suit ceiling panels, and miles of water pipes, as well, for a complete sprinkler system. Forty miles of conduits and electric wiring were installed as well as 2,100 special hand wrought fixtures.

Then followed finishes; thousands upon thousands of yards of gyproc, 23,000 square yards of craftex, 1,400 doors, 535 windows, 103-1/2 miles of wooden moulding, a vast quantity of finished flooring, 18,000 square feet of tile dado, and many other items too numerous to mention.
(SOURCE: Article "The Seigniory Club" by Architect Harold Lawson.)

LOG TECHNIQUES AT CHATEAU MONTEBELLO

The Operating Department of the Club has developed a technique of log construction that takes care of normal shrinkage. It is solid, permanent and satisfying. It is honest, for construction and finish are integral, within and without. With no inconsistency, comfort and convenience can be provided to suit any demand, as has been demonstrated in other cabins, all of which have stood up well with low maintenance. — Architect Harold Lawson, writing in "Le Seigneur", Summer 1944, p. 19.

VICTOR NYMARK
The Master Log Builder

"All log builders are my brothers" — Victor Nymark, speaking at the Log Structures of Canada Conference, Banff, Alberta, in October 1977.

Victor Nymark, the master log builder of the Chateau Montebello, is one of the unsung heroes of our day. So often the architects and engineers get all the credit. The man who *did the job,* who taught and supervised other men, who had to make decisions on the job and was often forced to work ahead of the arrival of blueprints because of a scheduled opening, deserves the recognition and the gratitude of every lover of log building.

God bless you, Victor Nymark, and thank you for a job well done!

THE PHOTOGRAPHS ON THE FOLLOWING PAGES
ARE A STEP-BY-STEP PICTORIAL PRESENTATION
OF THE HERCULEAN TASK OF BUILDING
THE CHATEAU MONTEBELLO.

Feb. 25, 1930. The construction staff. Victor Nymark did not join the staff until mid-March 1930.

Lucerne-in-Quebec, Community Association, Limited
Montebello, Que.
Photograph No....2
Date Taken ... Feb. 26th 1930
Title .... Hotel.

February 26, 1930. The site . . . the trees have been cut and the excess snow cleared away to make an early start possible in the spring.

Lucerne-in-Quebec Community Association, Ltd.
Montebello, Que.
Photograph No.... 5
Date Taken.... Feb. 26th 1930
Title..... Garage.

February 26, 1930. A steam shovel was used to dig the foundation of the garage. The site was extremely swampy and had to be drained.

BUILDING THE CHATEAU MONTEBELLO

Lucerne-in-Quebec Community Association, Ltd.
Montebello, Que.
Photograph No....7
Date Taken...Feb. 26.th 1930
Title....Garage.

The garage — stacks of panels for the concrete forms were ready to lay as soon as the excavation was completed.

March 17, 1930. The foundation walls of the garage
were partially completed.

Lucerne-in-Quebec Community Association Ltd
Montebello, Que.
Photograph..... No 11.
Date Taken ....March 17th
Title .... Garage.

*The bolts sticking up from the concrete walls were
ready to receive the logs.*

Lucerne-in-Quebec Community Association ltd.
Montebello, Que.
Photograph.... No. 12
Date Taken... March 17th
Title......Helps' Quarters.

March 17, 1930. The building site of Cedar Hall, the helps' quarters or staff house, also to be made of logs. The snow has been removed and the trees have been cut.

BUILDING THE CHATEAU MONTEBELLO

Lucerne-In-Quebec Community Assoc. Ltd.
Montebello - Que.
Photograph..... No 19.
Date Taken... April 3/30
Title.....Helps Quarters.

April 3, 1930. The form work for Cedar Hall (helps' quarters) was well underway. The site was like a swamp. Water was pumped away in the trough at the right. Boardwalks were needed everywhere.

April 3, 1930. The Hotel foundation and basements are well advanced. The stone arches are part of the future dining room.

BUILDING THE CHATEAU MONTEBELLO

Lucerne-In-Quebec Community Assoc. Ltd.
Montebello...Que.
Photograph No...21
Date Taken...April 3/30
Title...Cinder Track

April 3, 1930. In the early spring when the snow was melting you could hardly walk in from the main highway to the hotel site. To make it possible for trucks to come in, hundreds of loads of gravel and rocks were dumped and spread to make a road bed. The row of planks provided a track for wheel barrows.

Lucerne-In-Quebec Community Assoc. Ltd.
Montebello.. Que.
Photograph No.. 16
Date Taken... April 3/30
Title.... Garage.

April 3, 1930. The garage foundation was nearly completed. Note the old time steel-wheeled carts.

Lucerne in Quebec Community Ass'n
Montebello, Que.
Photograph No. 20
Date Taken...April 3/30
Title...Log Runway

April 3, 1930. The first load of logs resting on their railcars. The logs were unloaded onto this log run- *way for sorting. The elevated runways kept the logs clean and easier to lift.*

Lucerne-in-Quebec Community Assoc. Ltd.
Montebello - Que.
Photograph No... 22
Date Taken... April 15/30
Title... Hotel.

April 15, 1930. The first logs have been placed adjacent to the building.

BUILDING THE CHATEAU MONTEBELLO

Lucerne-in-Quebec Community Assoc. Ltd.
Montebello, Que.
Photograph No. 23
Date Taken... April 15/30
Title... Hotel

The first day of log construction. The tempo of the log work increased greatly within a few days with more men and round the clock operation.

Lucerne-in-Quebec Community Assoc. Ltd.
Montebello, Que.
Photograph No... 25
Date Taken... April 15/30
Title.....Helps Quarters

April 15, 1930. Cedar Hall floor system was laid.

April 15, 1930. The log work on the garage has been in progress for one week. The first log was laid April 7th for the garage.

Lucerne-in-Quebec Community Assoc Ltd.
Montebello, Que.
Photograph No... 28
Date Taken ..April 15/30
Title ....Garage.

April 15, 1930. The garage after nine days of log work. Each log has been mortised into vertical posts.

BUILDING THE CHATEAU MONTEBELLO

Lucerne-in-Quebec Community Assoc. Ltd.
Montebello Que.
Photograph No. 29
Date Taken...May 1/30
Title...End of Wing - Log Lodge

May 1, 1930. Twenty days after the log construction began one wing of the log lodge was nearly completed. The log alignment was perfect.

Lucerne-in-Quebec Community Assoc. Ltd
Montebello, Que.
Photograph No. 30
Date Taken...May 1/30
Title...Interior of Dining Room - Log Lodge

Only hand tools were used as skilled craftsmen trained men on the job to carve and fit each log to the one below it.

BUILDING THE CHATEAU MONTEBELLO

May 1, 1930. Picture taken twenty days after log work started on the hotel. The scene is the end of one of the wings. The entrance is made prominent *by the log post braces and rafters, all from round logs. Note the spline on the side of the window on the top floor. The spline fits into the groove in the* *end of the logs and allows for shrinkage. The window form is nailed onto the spline to hold it in place and still allow for shrinkage of the logs.*

Lucerne -in- Quebec Community Assoc. Ltd
Montebello Que
Photograph No... 32
Date Taken .... May 1/30
Title ... Wing "B" - Log Lodge

May 1, 1930. The roof work has begun on one wing.

Lucerne-in-Quebec Community Assoc. Ltd.
Montebello, Que.
Photograph No. 33
Date Taken May 1/30
Title... Dining Room-Log Lodge

Log joists for the dining room balcony protrude over the stone foundation wall. A log builder armed with only ax and scribes gets on with the job.

Levelling the support posts for the end of a bedroom wing.

Lucerne-in-Quebec Community Assoc. Ltd.
Montebello, Que
Photograph No...35
Date Taken...May 1/30
Title...Portion of House...

May 1, 1930. Cedar Hall twenty days after log construction began. The roof rafters are nearly installed.

Lucerne-in-Quebec Community Assoc. Ltd.
Montebello, Que.
Photograph No... 36
Date Taken... May 1/30
Title... Wing "C" - Log Lodge

34

May 1, 1930. Wing "C" of the log lodge.

A view of the temporary bunkhouses for the construction crew (taken during a lunch break). Aside from the bunkhouses, the men were also provided with a recreation hall, mess hall and other facilities *necessary for their comfort and well-being. (These buildings were dismantled nearly overnight when the opening of the Chateau took place.)*

**BUILDING THE
CHATEAU MONTEBELLO**

Lucerne-in-Quebec Community Assoc. Ltd
Montebello, Que.
Photograph No....38
Date Taken....May 1/30
Title...End of Garage

32

May 1, 1930. The garage was nearly completed.

Within the photo:

Lucerne-in-Quebec Community Assoc. Ltd.
Montebello, Que.
Photograph No. 39
Date Taken May 1/30
le: End View of Wing - Log Lodge

Hand augers were used to drill holes for the hand-made wooden pegs. Later on spikes were used to *speed up the work. However the spikes were oiled and countersunk to avoid hanging up the logs.*

BUILDING THE CHATEAU MONTEBELLO

Lucerne-in-Quebec Community Assoc. Ltd.
Montebello, Que.
Photograph No... 40
Date Taken... May 1/30
Title... View of Rotunda - Log Lodge
36

May 1, 1930. This is the central core from which the six wings extend in all directions. The center is the base for the six-sided fireplace which was later erected. The massive wooden forms have been completed and the workmen were ready to pour the concrete. Steel rods reinforced the concrete beams and floor. Before the concrete floor was set, when the concrete was still soft, wood and firring strips were set into the concrete and then the oak flooring was laid on top.

BUILDING THE
CHATEAU MONTEBELLO

Lucerne-in-Quebec Community Assoc., Ltd.
Montebello, Que.
Photograph No...41
Date Taken...May 1/30
Title...End View of Wing - Log Lodge

Note the staggered butt ends of the logs. Each log was cut with an axe. The log tips were painted to give a decorative rustic appearance.

BUILDING THE CHATEAU MONTEBELLO

Lucerne-in-Quebec Community Assoc. Ltd.
Montebello, Que.
Photograph No...42
Date Taken...May 1/30
Title...View of Boiler Room - Log Lodge
35

May 1, 1930. This is the foundation of the boiler room. Note the small crane at the right used to lift building materials on to the scaffolds after which everything was lifted by hand. The crane kept circling the building all the time.

BUILDING THE CHATEAU MONTEBELLO

Lucerne-in-Quebec Community Assoc. Ltd.
Montebello, Que.
Photograph No. 43
Date Taken.. May 1/30
Title... Night Operations - Log Lodge

9

To meet the July 1st opening deadline the log work was carried on 24 hours a day. Spotlights illuminated the area at night.

Lucerne-in-Quebec Community Assoc. Ltd.
Montebello Que.
Photograph...No. 44
Date Taken..May 11/30
Title...Boiler Room

May 11, 1930. The boiler room wing walls were nearly completed. The boiler room was located in the basement to provide steam heat for entire com- *plex. The driveway through the wing is the main entrance to the lodge.*

BUILDING THE CHATEAU MONTEBELLO

May 11, 1930. Cedar Hall needed only a few windows and doors, final roofing and clean up.

May 11, 1930. The southwest wing was roofed over. The dining room wing at the right was well underway. Notice the fireplace rising in the background.

BUILDING THE CHATEAU MONTEBELLO

May 11, 1930. The southeast wing was covered with rafters. The dining room wing now at the left was progressing more slowly due to masonry constructing.

A section of vertical logs is being lifted. Careful scribing and cutting made each vertical log fit the *curve of the base log. The same procedure was followed to fit the top railing.*

BUILDING THE CHATEAU MONTEBELLO

May 22, 1930. Five hundred thousand handsplit cedar shakes set in the foreground. Wings B and E were nearly completed.

May 22, 1930. The laying of water and sewer pipes
for the Lodge was a major undertaking.

BUILDING THE CHATEAU MONTEBELLO

Lucerne-in-Quebec Community Assoc Ltd
Montebello Que.
Photograph.. No. 58
Date Taken.. May 22/30
Title... Pipe cutting with compressed air.

The sewer gang worked furiously. Pipe cutting was done on the job. Note the old time compressor.

Lucerne-in-Quebec Community Assoc. Ltd.
Montebello, Que.
Photograph..No..56
Date Taken...May 22/30
Title..Lag Screw arrangement to allow
or expansion or contraction

This lag screw was screwed into a log. It is intended to slide down between the two uprights, allowing even settlement on the log wall. Nymark said the washer should have been larger to make sliding easier.

Lucerne-in-Quebec Community Assoc. Ltd
Montebello, Que.
Photograph No. 59
Date Taken June 2/30
Title View of Hotel from River Bank

*June 2, 1930. The roofs have been shaked. Only the
dining room and main lobby remained incomplete.*

Setting the log rafters at the center was one of the most difficult jobs.

BUILDING THE CHATEAU MONTEBELLO

June 2, 1930. The dining room wing.
Note the log ends added to the lumber rafters.

Lucerne-in-Quebec Community Assoc.
Montebello, Que.
Photograph...No...63
Date Taken..June 2/30
Title..Unloading Yard for Logs

Four carloads of logs a day were unloaded at this site.

Lucerne-in-Quebec Community Assoc. Ltd
Montebello Que
Photograph..No. 64
Date..Taken...June 10/30
Title..Wings "C" and "D" Log Lodge Hotel

The roof structure over the lobby was the most difficult bit of log work.

Craftsmen swarmed over the massive central roof structure like ants on an anthill or bees building a hive. Nymark said this was the most difficult job of all. On the wing roof structures, lumber rafters were used to which log ends were attached for effect to match the real log rafters exposed in the central roof structure above the lobby.

BUILDING THE
CHATEAU MONTEBELLO

Lucerne-in-Quebec Community Assoc. Ltd.
Mont..bello, Que.
Photograph..No.. 65
Date Taken.. June 10/30
Title.. Dining Room Wing-Log Lodge Hotel

June 10, 1930. Roofing continued. The dining room fireplace was completed. Work continued on the central fireplace.

Lucerne-in-Quebec Community Assoc. Ltd
Montebello Que.
Photo No .... 66.
Date Taken ...June 23/30.
Title ...Wings "C" and "D". Log Lodge Hotel

*June 23, 1930. Landscaping and cleanup remained
around the main wings. A week remained until the
grand opening.*

BUILDING THE CHATEAU MONTEBELLO

June 23, 1930. The roof over the boiler room wing was nearly completed.

Lucerne-in-Quebec Community Assoc. Ltd
Montebello, Que.
Photo No - 68
Date Taken ... June 23/30.
Title - View of Log Lodge Hotel from River.

Huge fieldstones for use in building the fireplaces
were brought from miles around by local habitants
in their wooden horse-drawn carts.

BUILDING THE CHATEAU MONTEBELLO

Lucerne-in-Quebec Community Association Ltd.
Montebello, Que.
Photo No. . . . . . 69.
ate Taken . . . . June 23/30.
Title Wing "D" Log Lodge Hotel.

At the end of June 23, 1930.

Large logs that were left over from the log chateau
were saved to build the entrance gate by the main
highway. Nothing was wasted.

BUILDING THE CHATEAU MONTEBELLO

A gang of workmen take their lunch hour; their faces reflect the hard times.

Within the image: Lucerne-in-Quebec Commu...ty Assoc. Lta Montebello, Que. Photograph..No. ? Date Taken July 2nd/30 Title...Log Lodge General View of Wings C&D

Gaily-striped red and white awnings decorated every window in time for the Grand Opening, July 1, 1930.

BUILDING THE CHATEAU MONTEBELLO

PART THREE

Life at the Seigniory Club

At the Grand Opening on July 1, 1930, most of the guests may have arrived with preconceptions of log cabins associated with frontier posts, wilderness areas, and the hardships of pioneering and primitive living. Some perhaps envisioned "outhouses"! It was not that the Club and the news media had not prepared them for the splendid facilities which had been built, but ideas die hard and our ancestors had left us with a heritage of images of rude cabin construction. However, the Lucerne-in-Quebec Community Association Limited had seized on these ideas and developed and beautified them so that its members and guests could enjoy the romance of log cabin life, blended with the amenities of modern conditions.

One of the earliest visitors was the late famed newspaperman and humorist Gregory Clark, and he wrote: "Lucerne-in-Quebec is the last word in purely Canadian recreation. The people back of it have taken a vast hunk of the Laurentian hills, about halfway between Montreal and Ottawa, and have determined to create there something as gorgeously Canadian as Switzerland is gorgeously Swiss, or as Scotland is as gorgeously Scotch. The timber is to be preserved as if it were sacred relics. The hills blow with anemones in the early spring, and the trout abound in streams dammed by the beaver. Deer mince silently through its hardwood ridges and partridges cluck in the coverts. The immense Log Chateau, with all its appurtenant stables and garages, is the social core of the wide-flung estate. But through the valleys and on the hills are scattered the log cabins of the community of Lucerne.

"It is one of those dreams that came true in Switzerland and on the Riviera. And it looks as if it is coming true in Quebec. For it is bold, beautiful and clever."

The Grand Opening showed visitors a series of buildings, all of log construction, which were impressive in the extreme. They included the hotel, or Log Chateau, containing 186 rooms and baths as well as public rooms and a staff building. This latter, in itself, compares favorably in size with many a country hotel. The garage houses one hundred and fifty cars, providing space for repairing and cleaning, a hotel laundry, and accommodation for a score of men.

These were all now in use, while under construction was a sports pavilion of generous dimensions, an enclosed swimming pool and a large boat house.

The approach to the hotel property is through a log gate-lodge situated on the North Shore Montreal-Ottawa highway. Through a grove of ancient pines leads a broad private road, first straight, then gently curving, and in the bend revealing a huge log structure with roofs of hand-split shingles. The Log Lodge is built of French bow knot design. The walls are built of horizontal logs, notched at the corners and held in place at intervals of twenty-eight feet by log uprights. The logs average nine inches, and butts and tips alternate in order that the horizontal lines may be retained. The windows are casements painted green, and the logs are stained brown, which it was hoped would turn silvery grey after long exposure. (Frequent applications of stain, however, have kept the logs a dark brown color.)

The principal entrance to the hotel is gained through a covered driveway between the ball-room wing and the lounge. One enters a vestibule through a carved doorway with carved flanking wings directly into the lounge, an immense space in no dimension measuring less than one hundred feet across. Its dominating feature is the six-sided stone tower, with a fireplace on each side, in the centre of the lounge, which forms the focal point of convergence of the six wings.

Two galleries extend completely around the lounge and give access to the various corridors of the bedroom wings and to the ballroom. The lower gallery, called the mezzanine, is quite broad and, being furnished with couches and comfortable chairs commanding a view of the entire lounge, is popular as a sitting-out place. Two immense windows at the east and west ends admit adequate daylight and no more, and the absence of glare and the soft tones of the cedar log walls give this room an air of repose rather unexpected in view of its size.

We have mentioned Victor Nymark's difficulties with the roofing of this lounge and Architect Harold Lawson has also pointed out that "it was at once a challenge and an opportunity. We were very obviously limited by the length of the well-seasoned cedar logs that could be obtained within the limited time for construction. It was essential that everything be of logs and to employ a technique suited to logs with no hidden steel members or false structural effects. In this we would have succeeded had it not been decided, when our design was almost complete, to introduce steel tension members in the lounge roof framing, and also the roof trusses of the ballroom.

"As can be seen from the plan, the lounge is, roughly speaking, hexagonal in shape with but four sides of equal length. The main support of the roof depends on twenty-two log posts located on the inner line of the mezzanine with a continuous log plate over these posts taking the main rafters which radiate from the center. These being virtually cantilevers, the plate acts as a fulcrum. The small ends of the rafters are received on a timber collar encircling the chimney, and the butt ends are anchored to the wall plate which follows the outer perimeter of the lounge. Some of the radial rafters are sixty-eight feet long and measure twenty-four inches in diameter at the butt and upon these rest

long purlins of six-inch average diameter and about four feet apart, which, in turn, take the usual wooden rafters, double boarding, roof covering, furring and gypsum ceiling.

"There are, of course, numerous struts, ties and secondary members, all serving an essential structural function. No members have been introduced for effect, and the ensemble results in geometric patterns not without interest to the architect or engineer; in fact, the ceiling members in their relation to each other form a pattern not unlike an immense spider's web.

"The walls of the lounge are entirely structural. The construction is also the finish. One sees within the same logs as without, except that the inner side is left a natural color and varnished while all exterior logs are stained.

"Immediately below the lounge and conforming to it in general shape, but not in size nor architecture, is the grill room. It is a rough-plastered room containing thirteen large murals painted by Adam Sheriff Scott and has six large openings filled with iron grilles. The central portion contains a fountain within arcaded openings, the piers of which serve as supports for the four hundred and fifty ton lounge chimney.

"Filling the basement of one wing at the same level as the grill room are the tavern, billiard and card rooms. The tavern has walls of rubble stone, heavy adzed beams, straw-plastered ceiling and flagged floor, essentially a room for men.

"The main floor of the diningroom is also at this level, and together with its double-decked porches extending around three sides forms a complete wing in itself. On its plank floor three hundred diners may be accommodated with ease. Stone piers support a gallery which connects with the main floor of the lounge. From this gallery one gets an excellent view of twelve low relief painted panels of the coat-of-arms of Canada, the provinces and two territories by Adney. They are hexagonal in shape, set into the walls and give a happy relief to the logs which surround them. On this gallery are also two large murals by Scott representing two historical scenes of the Papineau Rebellion. The craftsman's touch is more evident here that in the lounge. The log terminations have been carved, lintels chamfered, logs converted to spiral columns and on the principal newel posts of the oak stair leading up to the lounge are the heads of a habitant and his wife carved by Trygg.

"The ballroom occupies a separate wing at the mezzanine level. It is approached by steps between carved posts, and at the opposite end is a stage framed within log carving beautifully done by craftsmen. All the carving, with the exception of the oak newel posts of the diningroom, was done by a small group of loggers with axe, drawknife and pocket knife. Nymark was one of these carvers.

"The ballroom was given a different finish to that of any of the other rooms, it being felt that its function called for more refined treatment, more in consonance with light entertainment and evening dress; and with this in view it was stained a silver grey and touched up with orange.

"The bedroom arrangement is the usual one common to most hotels in those days, with a small vestibule, within the corridor door, formed between the closet and bathroom. The partitions are sound-proof being virtually double on staggered studs and having four thicknesses of wall-board. Walls and ceiling are divided into panels, with rounded battens forming the stiles and rails. The wallboard is treated with plastic paint blending in color with the carpet and hangings of the room.

"As part of the great project the time-honored Chateau Papineau has been restored to its former state of splendor and is now the Seigniory Club. The historic atmosphere has been retained, but sufficient alterations have been made to the building to render it one of the finest club houses in Canada. A rustic pavilion, with refreshment service, for year round use, was built near the first tee of the golf course, while near it are swimming pool, tennis courts, toboggan chute, ski jump and skating rink. Within a short distance is a modern airport, the landing field of which is large, level and well drained. Between three and four miles of roadways have been built giving access to vacation sites."

The Log Lodge is open year round to accommodate summer and winter sports. The property was bought by the Canadian Pacific Railway Company in 1929 in an associated arrangement with a private club called Lucerne-in-Quebec Community Association Limited. Directors in 1930 were H. M. Saddlemire, President; the Hon. L. A. Taschereau, Premier of the Province of Quebec; E. W. Beatty, K. C., Chairman and President of the Canadian Pacific Railway Company; Hon. Frederick L. Beique, K. C., President of the Banque Canadienne Nationale; Sir Charles Gordon, G.B.E., President, Bank of Montreal; and Sir Herbert Holt, President, Royal Bank of Canada. In 1971, the Canadian Pacific Hotels bought the entire property but all members still retain certain rights and privileges.

It is interesting to note the rights and privileges enjoyed by members when the club opened in 1930.

First: A Charter Life Membership in Lucerne-in-Quebec Seigniory Club, free from the payment of any initiation fee or annual dues. This membership carried full privileges for dependent members of the family, including their right to use freely the golf course, tennis courts, swimming and many other recreational facilities, without payment of golf and other fees.

Second: A Lucerne-in-Quebec Seigniory Club member, in case he transfers his homesite, may resign and cause the election of the transferee, provided the latter is acceptable to the Board of Governors. Upon the death of a member his homesite will in like manner qualify an acceptable successor for membership.

Third: Ownership of 10,000 square feet of land (one subdivision) upon which a home may be built. No notarial or recording fees are payable in connection with the warranty deed.

Fourth: The Log Chateau club rates for rooms are available to Members and their dependent families. These rates are ten per cent below the rates charged to ordinary members, guests, or persons introduced by members.

Fifth: The association will submit, upon request of a member, a variety of building plans and cost estimates for the construction of a home. In general, all private structures are restricted to log cabin or Swiss chalet type.

Sixth: The services and facilities of the construction and interior decorating departments of Lucerne-in Quebec Community Association Limited, at reasonable costs, for the construction, equipment and furnishing of the homes.

Seventh: Exclusive club fishing and hunting privileges on an enormous game preserve, in the heart of Canada's game country.

The original club directors are dead now and many changes have taken place in the rights and privileges. For instance, it is now permitted to build a house of other material than log. There are also different types of memberships — Charter, Life, Term and Ordinary, each with its own initiation dues and annual fees.

With the passage of time and changes in economic conditions, this is inevitable. However, the aims of the Seigniory Club (the name Lucerne-in-Quebec was dropped many years ago) remain much the same through Canadian Pacific Hotels owns most of the property with Charter members owning their own individual properties.

Not the least of the benefits enjoyed by members of the Seigniory Club is careful and constant protection. Police and Fire Departments, also Woods and Guides sections, extend into the wilderness over the 104 square miles of the Club's territory. The Woods Department guards against poachers and fire, improves the value of the timber by proper silvicultural methods,

maintains the miles of highways and trails and keeps in good order forty-one miles of forest telephone line. All rangers are special constables.

The Guides Department looks after the pleasure and health of the members when they are in the forest. They conduct parties on hiking, canoeing, fishing, hunting, and motor boat trips. Members of the Police Department are sworn in as special constables. Their role today is not quite as stern as it used to be when they demanded proper credentials before admitting anyone to the Seigniory Club grounds.

At one time there were 1,500 members of the Club but it is believed this number has dwindled to about 400. But they have included the blue bloods of Canada and other countries and their guests. Some of the more prominent have been Queen Juliana of the Netherlands, Prince Rainier and Princess Grace of Monaco, former Prime Minister Lester Pearson, the late Bing Crosby and Perry Como were particularly addicted to the Montebello golf course, and other world-famous personalities from Canada and the United States have stayed there. The membership list includes a princess, politicians, bankers, lawyers, doctors and company presidents from the U.S., France, England, Switzerland and the Bahamas.

Every recreational desire and need seems to have been anticipated in the creation of this unusual playplace in the midst of the storied Province of Quebec.

Keeping as an ideal the conservation and preservation of the natural beauties so abundant in this region, roads, sports facilities, water and sewer systems, and all other requisites have been laid out in such a way that the charm of the forest, waters and mountains can be maintained for all time. New buildings, whenever and wherever erected, will blend harmoniously into their sylvan settings, for all will be of wooden, though not necessarily of log construction.

Lucerne-in-Quebec Community Assoc.
Montebello, Que.   Ltd.
Photograph..No..83
Date Taken..July 14th/30
Title..Log Lodge-Hotel

Visitors never tire of walking around the Chateau.

Umbrella table and chair sets invite guests to sit and
contemplate.

BUILDING THE CHATEAU MONTEBELLO

Dining Room Wing, Rock Gardens and Flagged Terrace, Log Chateau

Grass terraces provide a restful setting for afternoon teas.

Beautifully landscaped terraces provide restful places for quiet talks or reflection.

BUILDING THE CHATEAU MONTEBELLO

A Log Chateau Bedroom Wing, showing notched log construction.

Spacious and airy suites command excellent views of the Ottawa River. How many clubs or hotels can boast of such elegance?

BUILDING THE CHATEAU MONTEBELLO

Lucerne-in-Quebec Community Assoc. Lt
Montebello, Que.
Photograph No. 76
Date Taken July 2nd/30
Title Progress View Entrance Gates to

July 2. Work commences on the log gate house which Nymark built with the large butt ends of left-over logs.

BUILDING THE CHATEAU MONTEBELLO

Lucerne-in-Quebec Community Assoc. Ltd.
Montebello, Que.
Photograph No. 85
Date Taken July 14th./30
Title Log Lodge Showing Entrance from West

The latest models were always to be found at the Montebello. The rail spur has since been removed.

Lucerne-in-Quebec Community Assoc.Ltd.
Montebello, Que.
Photograph No.... 100.
Date Taken ...Aug. 7/30.

Title... Main Entrance to Log Lodge Hotel.

*A guest's vintage car arrives in beautifully
decorated Main Entrance.*

Main Entrance, The Log Lodge.

Main Entrance. The entranceway is beautifully protected from the weather. The windows above are the theater/ballroom windows. Victor Nymark was *personally responsible for the elaborate wood carving on the posts. Note the decorative effect of the handhewed squared beam across the entranceway.*

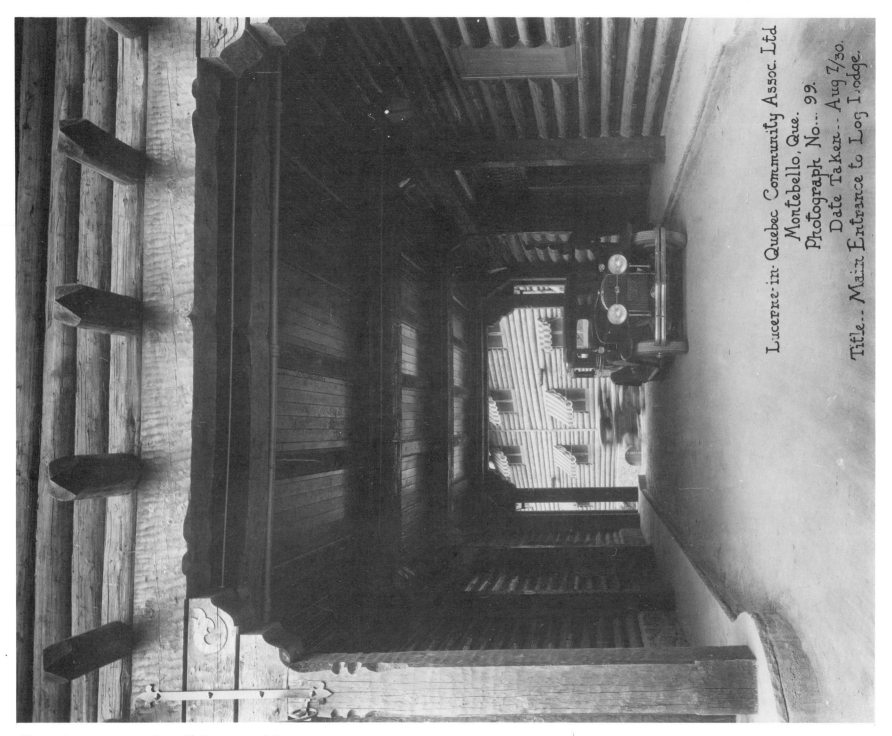

Lucerne-in-Quebec Community Assoc. Ltd
Montebello, Que.
Photograph No.. 99.
Date Taken.. Aug 7/30.

Title.. Main Entrance to Log Lodge.

*The main entrance was beautifully protected from
the weather.*

Within the photograph:

Lucerne in Quebec Community Assoc. Ltd.
Montebello, Que.
Photograph No.. 96.
Date Taken.... July 1930
Title, Fireplace seen from Entrance Log Lodge

The visitors' first glimpse of the lobby as seen from the entrance.

The six-sided fireplace towering to 66 feet is a stunning piece of workmanship. Victor Nymark also helped with the fireplace.

Another view of the Main Lounge, Log Chateau

A view of the lobby from the first balcony.

BUILDING THE CHATEAU MONTEBELLO

Lucerne-in-Quebec Community Assoc.Ltd
Montebello, Que.
Photograph No.. 94
Date Taken -- July 19/30
Title : General view Dining Room

The dining room from the balcony adjacent to the lobby. The area behind the fireplace is an enclosed *sunporch overlooking the Ottawa River. The sunporch borders the dining room on three sides.*

BUILDING THE CHATEAU MONTEBELLO

Hooded Fireplace, Mezzanine Level, Log Chateau Dining Room.

A quiet corner. . . a spot-to-relax balcony above the dining room. The doors lead to the enclosed sun- porch. Shields on the walls are of the various pro- vinces.

BUILDING THE CHATEAU MONTEBELLO

The Log Chateau Dining Room

This view of the dining room looks toward the lobby. Note the massive fireplace beyond the center balconies.

BUILDING THE CHATEAU MONTEBELLO

Carved Newel Posts and Entrance to Lounge from Dining Room Log Lodge

Dining Room Balcony. Delicately carved posts add real finesse to the log balcony.

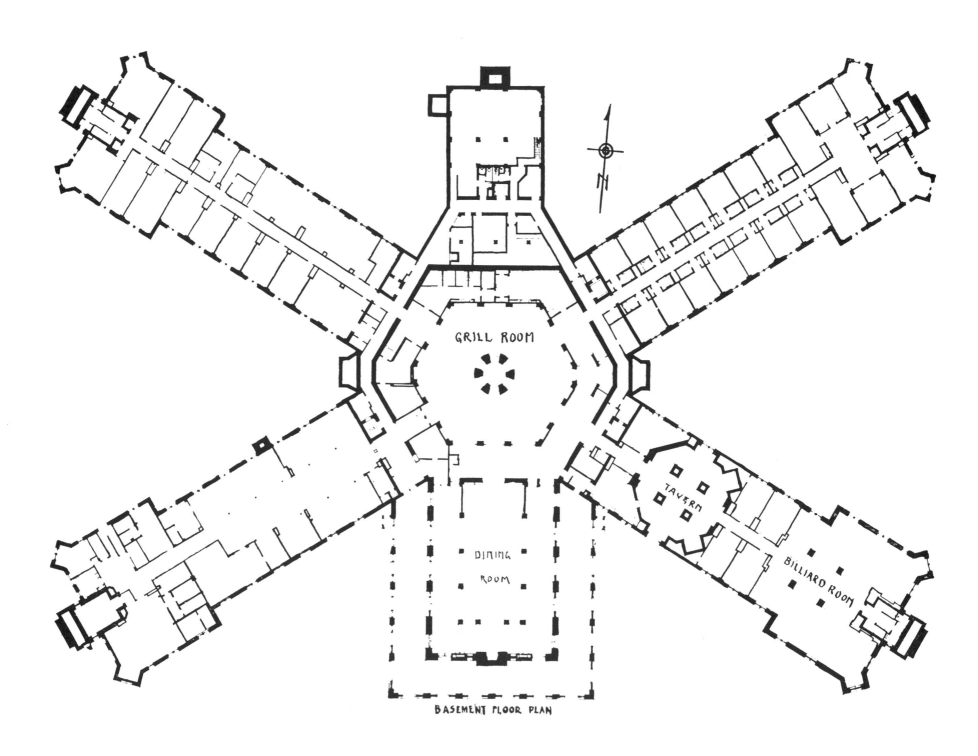

GRILL ROOM

DINING

ROOM

TAVERN

BILLIARD ROOM

BASEMENT FLOOR PLAN

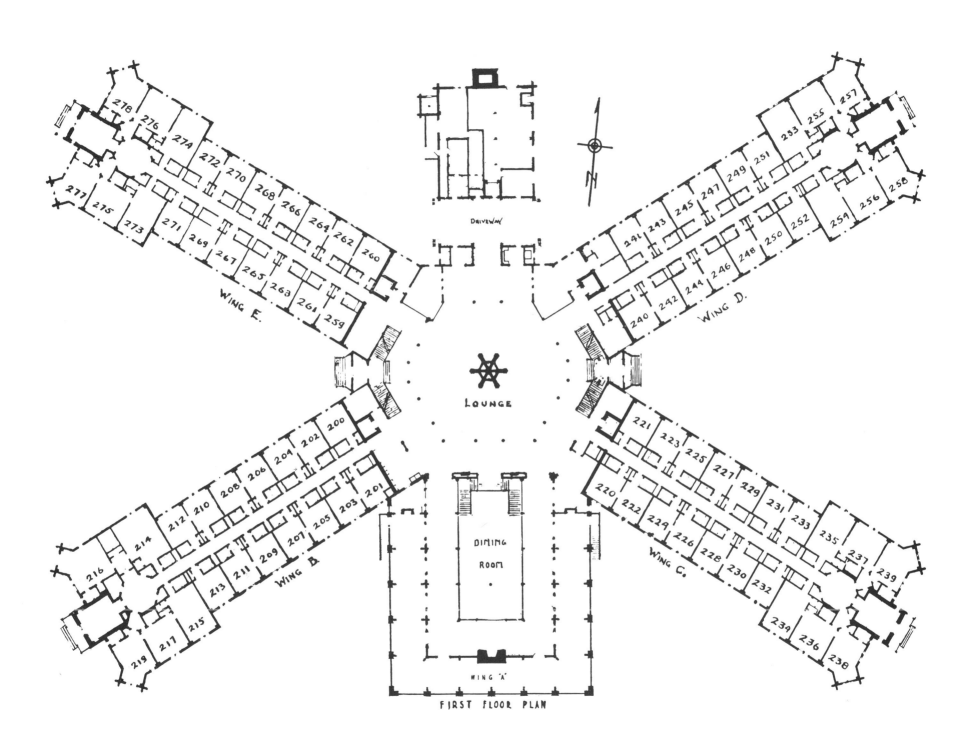

DRIVEWAY

WING E.

WING D.

LOUNGE

WING B.

DINING ROOM

WING C.

WING "A"

FIRST FLOOR PLAN

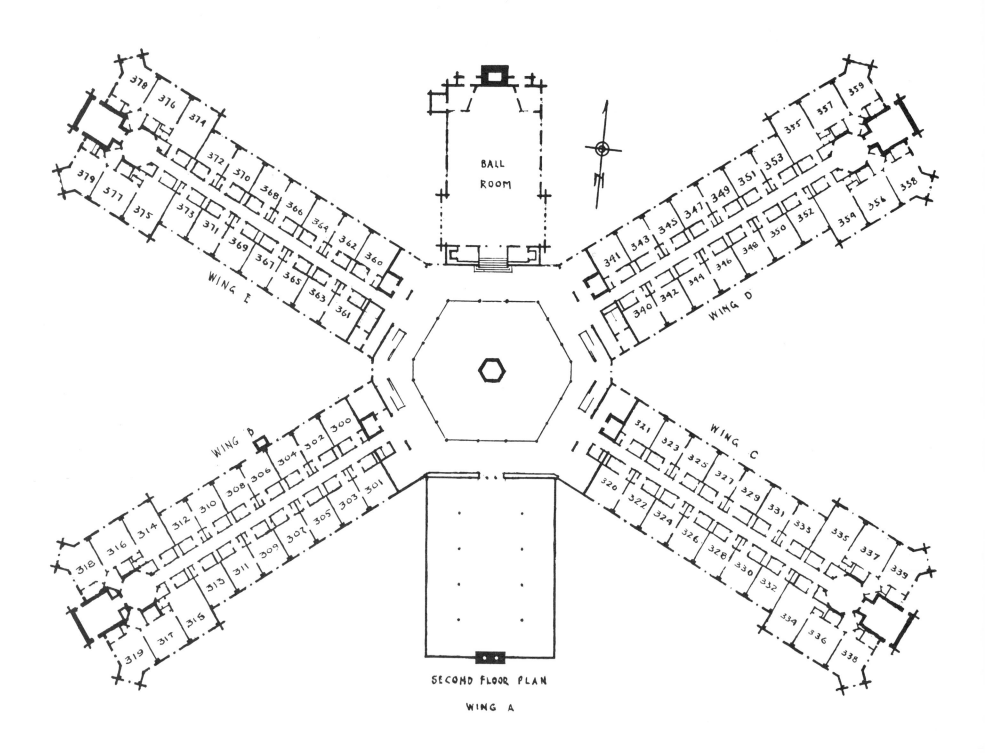

BALL ROOM

WING E

WING D

WING B

WING C

SECOND FLOOR PLAN

WING A

BUILDING THE CHATEAU MONTEBELLO

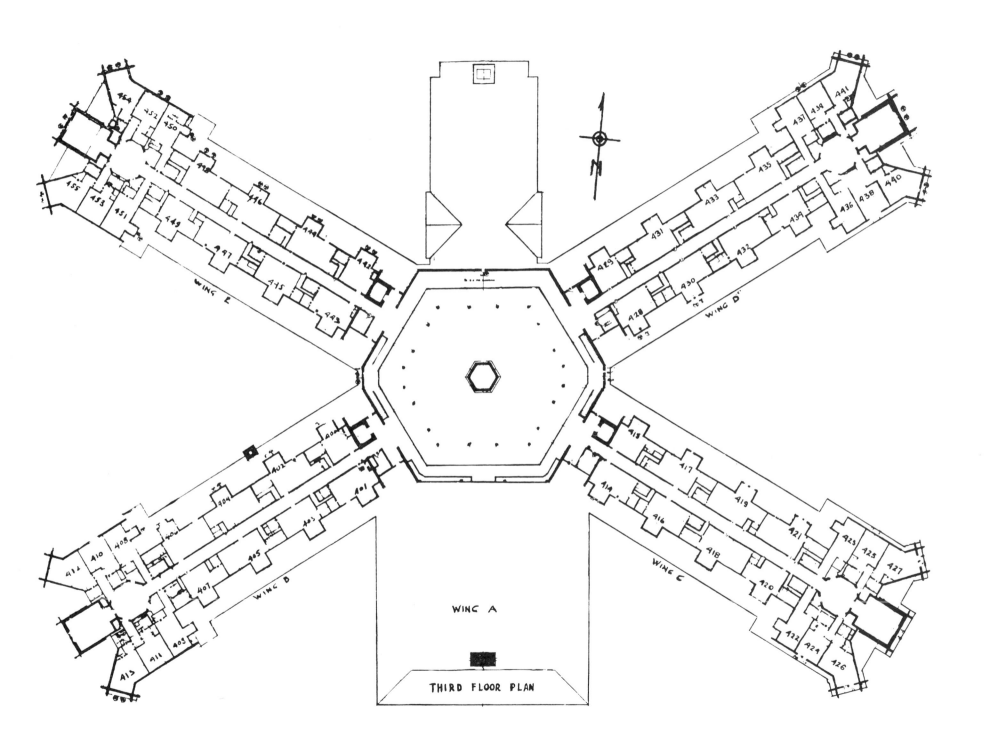

THIRD FLOOR PLAN

WING A

WING B

WING C

WING D

WING E

BUILDING THE CHATEAU MONTEBELLO

Lucerne-in-Quebec Community Assoc. Ltd
Montebello Que.
Photograph No. 93.
Date Taken - July 19/30
Title. A Typical Suite

The log chateau bedrooms were spacious and well furnished. Each room had its own tile bathroom.

Lucerne-in-Quebec Community Assoc Ltd
Montebello, Que.
Photograph No. 92
Date Taken .. July 29/30
Title.. A Typical Bedroom.

Many of the bedrooms are adjoined by comfortable sitting rooms. Note the carved and painted woodwork on the beds.

The tavern. Today, it's a coffee shop.

BUILDING THE CHATEAU MONTEBELLO

Lucerne in Quebec Community Assoc. Ltd
Montebello Que.
Photograph No. 89.
Date Taken .. July 19/30
Title .. Central Section. Griil Room.

The Grill Room was located beneath the Main Lobby. In the center of the room there was an arched stone fountain with a pool lined with faience tile.

The stone pillars helped to support the great fireplace in the lobby. The walls of the Grill Room bore historic murals.

BUILDING THE CHATEAU MONTEBELLO

Lucerne-in-Quebec Community Assoc. Ltd.
Montebello, Que.
Photograph No.. 88.
Date Taken.. July 19/30.
Title.. Log Lodge, showing Kitchen.

The Log Chateau kitchen was well equipped and ex-
pertly staffed.

Log Chateau Billiard Room.

The Billiard Room had a cork floor, easy chairs, and the facilities for chess and checkers.

Lucerne-in-Quebec Community Assoc Ltd
Montebello, Que.
Photograph No...95.
Date Taken ... July 19/30.
Title.. The Ballroom at Log Lodge

The Log Chateau ballroom doubles as a theater. Note the roof structure.

July 2, 1930. Cedar Hall was finished and occupied by hotel staff.

Lucern̄... Quebec Community Assoc. Ltd.
Montebello, Que.
Photograph..No.. 75.
Date Taken..July 2nd/30
Title.. The Garage

The 200-car garage as it appeared at the opening. Note the precision log work at the gable ends. All logs were scribe fitted to the diagonal supports of the roof system.

Interior of the Log Lodge Garage.

The roof structure of the garage is a masterpiece.

Entrance to Log Chateau Garage.

Only one-third of the garage complex is visible here.

Lucerne-in-Quebec Community Assoc. Ltd.
Montebello, Que
Photograph..No.. 119
Date Taken..Dec. 6th 1930
Title..Freight Shed

The freight shed was built during the fall of 1930.

Lucerne-in-Quebec Community Assoc. Ltd.
Montebello Que.
Photograph: No 103
Date Taken.. Aug. 7/30
Title: Log Station

The Log Station at Montebello under construction.
Many visitors arrived at the Chateau by train. In
the winter they were transported from the station
by horse and sleigh, or even a dog sled.

BUILDING THE CHATEAU MONTEBELLO

They came by train and ski-plane, by sleigh and dog sleds, to participate in all winter sports.

BUILDING THE CHATEAU MONTEBELLO

An invitation to reflection.

The Pioneers' Club meeting room. The Pioneers' Club was composed of Seigniory Club members who were the first to build cabins on their property. The furniture shown here was made of logs by club carpenters.

BUILDING THE CHATEAU MONTEBELLO

The Sports Club is of log and stone construction. It serves as a golf and country club house in summer; a club for skiers in the winter. The one-and-a-half storey club house is 60 x 71 ft. at the center, with two wings each 58 x 29 ft.

The Swimming Pool is 75 x 40 ft. with a depth of 12 ft. by the diving tower. It is enclosed in a log building measuring 150 x 91 ft. At night, there are colored submarine lights below the surface. The building contains a reception room, as well as the usual locker rooms and showers. It is heated in the winter by the oil furnaces in the Log Chateau.

The Boat House at the marina.

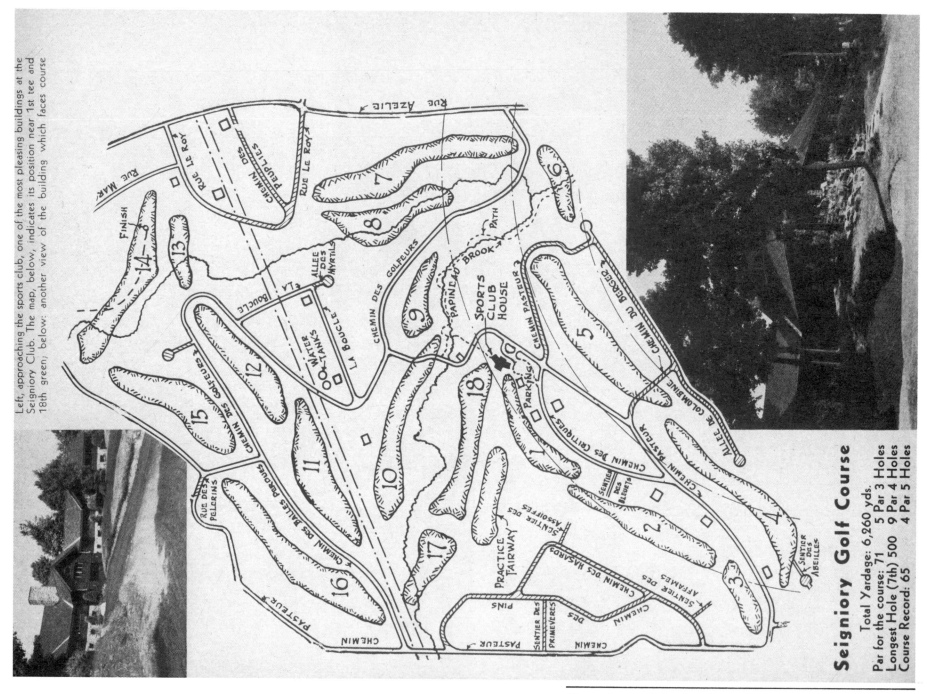

Left, approaching the sports club, one of the most pleasing buildings at the Seigniory Club. The map, below, indicates its position near 1st tee and 18th green; below: another view of the building which faces course

Seigniory Golf Course

Total Yardage: 6,260 yds.
Par for the course: 71   5 Par 3 Holes
Longest Hole (7th) 500   9 Par 4 Holes
Course Record: 65   4 Par 5 Holes

Illustration and photo credit: Le Seigneur, Summer 1949, p. 10.

Lucerne-in-Quebec Community Assoc. Ltd.
Montebello, Que.
Photograph No. 118
Date Taken Nov. 22nd 1930
Title. Golf Course

This golf course has been carved out of the forest on the lower slopes of Westcott Mountain. View is one of the thirteenth fairway.

Breakfast at Cranberry Cabin, near Cranberry Lake. Fully equipped guides were available to *members for hunting, fishing, and camping throughout the hundred-square-mile forest.*

The fish hatchery at Whitefish Lake, completed in December 1931. It is 73 x 25 feet and includes living quarters, office, ice room, trough room, and feed room. It is heated by a hot air furnace.

Dancers at the Christmas Ball.

The curling club occupies the east wing of the garage.

BUILDING THE CHATEAU MONTEBELLO

The resident Fire Department not only protected the Chateau and its environs but was also on call to assist the village of Montebello.

The Protective Service included a small police force to patrol the grounds day and night. Rangers and guides took care of the forest lands and their visitors.

The first snow, as glimpsed through a Club window, brings a new and very beautiful world into being. At the Seigniory Club it heralds one of the most attractive and stimulating of seasons in this part of *Canada when skiing, skating, tobogganing, sleighing, curling and all the other winter sports flourish. (Photo credit: Max Sauer, Montreal).*

BUILDING THE CHATEAU MONTEBELLO

Passing through the Main Entrance is a soul-stirring experience. For the new visitor it is only the first taste of grandeur.

J. G. Stenhouse, left, with Mr. and Mrs. R. C. Ronalds, Montreal, arrive in winter furs en route to Manor.

Local color at the Seigniory Club were these dog-team driven sledges.

BUILDING THE CHATEAU MONTEBELLO

Lucerne-in-Quebec Community Assoc. ltd
Montebello, Que.
Photograph No. 127
Date Taken..Dec 6th 1930
Title..Bobsleigh Run

*The mile-long bobsled run was completed for use by
the winter of 1930-31.*

BUILDING THE CHATEAU MONTEBELLO

A skating rink in winter; the tennis courts in summer.

With an ice wall breaking the wind the winter sun is warm and enjoyable in the Club's outside solarium.

BUILDING THE CHATEAU MONTEBELLO

A view from the ski jump.

BUILDING THE CHATEAU MONTEBELLO

The ski jump. 34,000 cubic yards of rock and earth were taken from the hillside to provide the correct grading of the landing slope. 100 tons of steelwork hold the top platform 143 feet in the air — the tallest ski chute in the world (1931) — with the top of the tower 301 feet above the level of the final run.

BUILDING THE
CHATEAU MONTEBELLO

That's a lot of log work!

BUILDING THE CHATEAU MONTEBELLO

Some of the original Seigniory Club members examining the new ski jump built in the Fall of 1930.

Skiers in 1930 ski gear — high fashion in those days! Note the bamboo ski poles and wooden skis.

BUILDING THE CHATEAU MONTEBELLO

The entire area is a cross-country skier's paradise.

The ice-skating rink was surrounded by walls of packed snow.

BUILDING THE CHATEAU MONTEBELLO

Ski-joring. The be-all and end-all of winter sports at the Seigniory Club.

Epilogue

"Keeping as an ideal the conservation and preservation of the natural beauties so abundant in this region, roads, sports facilities, water and sewer systems, and all other requisites have been laid out in such a way that the charm of the forests, waters and mountains will be maintained for all time." — Lucerne-in-Quebec Community Association Limited, 1930.

The Chateau Montebello attracts many different kinds of visitors. Although it was built as a rich man's playground and place of retreat, it is now a CP Hotel, open to the public.

It is still the home of the Seigniory Club whose membership is steadily increasing. The Club has just celebrated the 50th anniversary of the Grand Opening which took place on July 1, 1930.

With the widest possible range of recreational pursuits to be found anywhere in the world, the Chateau Montebello is not only attracting great numbers of individual guests but a steady stream of convention and conference gatherings. The sylvan setting and natural beauty contribute to any activity.

In recent years, with the advent of a log building renaissance throughout the continent of North America, the reputation of the Log Chateau as the world's largest log structure has spread.

Today, the Chateau Montebello is a kind of log builder's mecca, a shrine to which every true log enthusiast must journey. At least one time he or she should stand before those strong walls and, in the silence, hear the million blows of axes which built this wondrous lodge.

Log builders of today should let these walls be a standard by which their own work might be judged. They should also know that beyond the vision, the money, the excellent log work, were the men — hardworking men, unemployed men, distressed men, *but men who could work as a team.* Nothing else but teamwork could have built such a place.

We are in a dangerously similar economic plight today with inflation, recession and unemployment.

More log structures could be built, not only for recreation, but for habitation, education, and commercial establishments.

In North America, we have the trees. To what better use could they be put? Whole villages could be built quickly and economically with very little disturbance to the environment. We have the trained and experienced log builders. Who will hire them?

Perhaps we need a few more men of vision. . . a few more craftsmen *working as a team. . .*

An over-the-shoulder view for visitors driving away. . . bearing fond memories . . . and a promise to return again and again.

BUILDING THE CHATEAU MONTEBELLO

Bibliography

Le Seigneur, published by the Seigniory Club, Montebello. (Bound volumes of the Seigniory Club magazine for many years.)

Le Chateau Montebello, published by Canadian Pacific Hotels. (Brochure).

Construction, August 1930. (Magazine).

The Journal, published by the Royal Architectural Institute of Canada, January 1931. (Magazine).

Louis-Joseph Papineau: A Divided Soul, by Fernand Ouellet. Published by The Canadian Historical Association. Historical booklet No. 11.

The Log Lodge, Lucerne-in-Quebec, published by Lucerne-in-Quebec Community Association Limited, 1930. (Brochure).

Lucerne-in-Quebec, published by Lucerne-in-Quebec Community Association Limited, 1930. (Brochure).

Seigniory Club, Lucerne-in-Quebec, published by Lucerne-in-Quebec Community Association Limited, 1931. (Brochure).

Annual Report of the Seigniory Club, 1931, published by the Seigniory Club, Lucerne-in-Quebec. (Brochure).

Log Home Guide for Builders and Buyers, 1978, published by Muir Publishing Company Limited. Article on pp. 2-10, "Log Home Guide Pays Tribute to Victor Nymark". (Magazine).

Also available through Muir Publishing Company Ltd.
Publishers of the Log Home Guide for Builders & Buyers

BUILDING WITH LOGS, by B. Allan Mackie. The indispensable textbook for anyone even remotely interested in log building. Profusely illustrated and written by a man deeply committed to handcrafted log buildings. A standard textbook in most log building courses. 76 pps. Hardcover $25.00; softcover $16.

NOTCHES OF ALL KINDS, by B. Allan Mackie. Master log builder Mackie describes all the notches and joints used in log construction with an explanation of the special function of each. Lavishly illustrated with step-by-step diagrams and photographs. Like Mackie's other books, a must for the serious log builder. 90 pps. $16.

LOG HOUSE PLANS, by Allan Mackie. The latest book by the guru of handcrafted log builders. 37 complete Mackie house plans and an excellent introduction giving recommendations for a Survival Lifestyle. Appendices on construction, finishing and preserving. A must for every builder and buyer. 172 pps. Softcover $16.

THE TIMBER FRAMING BOOK, by S. Elliott & E. Wallas. A must for anyone interested in timberframe structure. Profusely illustrated with accurate professional drawings and dozens of on-the-job action photographs. 169 pp. $13.95 ($15.95 in Canada).

LOG BUILDING TOOLS & HOW TO MAKE THEM, by R. D. Arcand. Do it yourself and save hundreds of dollars. A guide and inspiration to those with the inclination to make their own tools. Describes many tools which are hard to find today. Profusely illustrated. 64 pps $6.95.

LOG STRUCTURES: PRESERVATION AND PROBLEM-SOLVING, by Harrison Goodall and Renee Friedman. Practical, detailed instructions for dealing with the difficulties in log constructions – wood decay, loose chinking, leaking roofs and sagging floors. Chapters cite measures for salvaging, and provide guidance in planning restoration with specific techniques for preserving. Some 93 photographs and 57 diagrams illustrate how to accomplish each step. With this book, new life is assured to thousands of historic log structures urgently in need of rescue – and healthier life to their modern counterparts. 119 pages. $10.95 ($12.95 in Canada).

THE COMPLETE LOG HOUSE BOOK, by Dale Mann and Richard Skinulis. Photography by Nancy Shanoff. A beautifully illustrated and inspiring book covering all aspects of design and construction of the four methods of log building: hewn, long log, piece-on-piece and stackwall. Valuable information on planning, materials, tools, techniques, insulation, wood preservatives, and much more. An essential textbook for all builders. 176 pps. $12.95 ($14.95 in Canada).

BUILDING THE TIMBER FRAME HOUSE, by Ted Benson with James Gruber. Illustrations by Jamie Page. Written by the owner of a post-and-beam construction firm in New Hampshire and a civil engineer, this book tells exactly how to build a timber frame house. Beginning with a brief, interesting chapter on the history of timber framing, the authors include chapters on the kinds of joinery, the assembly of timbers and raising. The last part of the book deals with present-day design and materials: house plans, site development, foundation-laying, insulation, tools and methods. $13.95 ($16.95 in Canada).

THE ENERGY ECONOMICS AND THERMAL PERFORMANCE OF LOG HOUSES, by Muir-Osborne. For years, the *Log Home Guide for Builders & Buyers* has been gathering data and supporting research on the energy-efficiency of log homes. This material now confirms the superiority of the log home and it's documented in this book written by the *Log Home Guide*'s editorial staff. $5.

YOUR LOG HOUSE, by Vic Janzen. The most comprehensive textbook yet written on how to build your own log house. With frequent references to a simple house plan, master craftsman Vic Janzen follows a step-by-step, cumulative approach to building. Janzen is careful to spell out possible problems and to caution first-time builders about any delusions or preconceived notions they may bring to a project. Interior stud wall framing, electrical work, heating, mathematics of roof building, use of subtrades, are also dealt with. 169 pps., 140 + line drawings and almost as many photographs. $15.00.

BUILDING THE ALASKA LOG HOME, Tom Walker. "I doubt there is another book in the market that would inspire one to build like this one does. The photography, all of it in color, is superb. Walker includes many examples of appealing buildings in a great variety of designs, from the trappers cabin to the elegant log home in suburbia. The design principles articulate the excellence. Walker's love for his work shines through. If his buildings are as handcrafted as his book, he is a man to be admired. This book is certainly a welcome addition to my building library and I am pleased to recommend it." – Vic Janzen, author of 'Your Log House'. 178 pages. Softcover $19.95 ($23.95 Can.).

BEFORE YOU BUILD: A PRECONSTRUCTION GUIDE, Robert Roskind. This book is a must for those planning to build their own log home (or any home for that matter). Using a checklist/questionnaire format, Roskind outlines what questions need to be answered and helps the do-it-yourselfer organize his construction schedule in the most efficient way. The book asks questions such as, "Is there good southern exposure for passive or active solar use? What is the zoning on the land? Does the land welcome

you?" Instead of thinking "Hmm...I should have thought of that earlier" when a problem crops up, this volume will help the owner/builder avoid potential pitfalls. 149 pp., checklists and illustrations. Softcover $7.95 (Can. $8.95).

STAV OG LAFT I NORGE, Early Wooden Architecture in Norway, Gunnar Bugge and Christian Norberg-Schultz. The first comprehensive work on the folk-architecture of Norway. The authors have selected about 60 representative examples illustrating the different types of farms, farm houses and stave-churches, and have treated the historical and artistic development in a general introduction. The book has 168 large pages and over 400 illustrations. Text is in Norwegian and English. Hardcover $27.50 ($35.00 Can.)

THE CRAFT OF LOG BUILDING, Hermann Phleps. Now translated from the German, this outstanding book is the most important volume on log building available in the northern hemisphere. A classic in Germany *The Craft of Log Building* is the master work of Hermann Phleps, whose career as an architect and teacher of the art of timberwork spanned nearly 60 years. *The Craft of Log Building* includes 419 drawings and photographs. Some of Phleps' examples of wood craftsmanship far exceed the purely ornamental and can only be described as exceptional artistry. 328 pp., 11" by 8-1/2" Softcover $19.95.

THE BOOK OF MASONRY STOVES, David Lyle. The masonry stove, widely used in Europe and Asia for centuries, surmounts many of the serious problems associated with wood heat and iron stoves: chimney fires, air pollution, poor energy efficiency. *The Book of Masonry Stoves* is the first comprehensive survey of all the major types of masonry heating systems, ancient and modern. Detailed plans and building information are included in the book. "Readers will find it hard to leave the book without having an overwhelming desire to install one of these wonderfully efficient, sensible devices in their home," writes Richard Ketchum, editor of Blair & Ketchum's *Country Journal*. 192 pages. Full of illustrations. Softcover $14.95 ($18.75 Can.)

HOW TO AFFORD YOUR OWN LOG HOME, Carl Heldmann. This book explains how you can build your own log home and save a lot of money by acting as your own contractor. Each step in the building process is examined, together with pitfalls, so that you can surmount the problems on your own. We feel it is an indispensable guide for the beginning builder who needs instructions about the Who, What, Why, When, Where and How of dealing with local tradesmen, building officials, banks and the whole complicated subject of erecting a house. We wish it had been in print before we started building! 137 pages, many photographs, charts, forms, etc. Softcover $9.95 ($12.95 Can.)

LOG HOME DESIGN, by the editorial staff of *Log Home Guide* **magazine.** Forty-seven log house plans representing various design trends, also feature articles on how to design a log home, environmental design, and traditional principles and contemporary design. $3.00.

THE HANDBOOK OF CANADIAN LOG BUILDING, F. Dan Milne. This comprehensive book by builder–designer–instructor Dan Milne is a basic step-by-step learning course in log construction. Superbly illustrated with full color photos, precise line drawings, and flow-through charts. *The Handbook of Canadian Log Building* is designed for use by anyone in the log building industry, novice or professional. It is also intended to provide a useful reference book for building authorities and teaching institutions. The author has had a decade of log building experience, is founder of the British Columbia School of Log Building, and is the Canadian expert whose advice was sought in establishing the School of Canadian Log Building in Japan. $24.95.

Readers interested in any of these titles may obtain further information from the Log Home Guide Mail Order Book-Log, Muir Publishing Co. Ltd., 1 Pacific, Ste. Anne de Bellevue, Que., Canada H9X 1BO, (or) Muir Publishing Co. Ltd., P.O. Box 1150, Plattsburgh, NY 12901. Credit card users may call toll-free: 1-800-345-LOGS (USA), 1-800-624-7214 (TENNESSEE); in Canada (514) 457-2045.